Edward O. Skelton

Historical review of the Boston Bijou Theatre:

With the original casts of all the operas that have been produced at the

Bijou

Edward O. Skelton

Historical review of the Boston Bijou Theatre:
With the original casts of all the operas that have been produced at the Bijou

ISBN/EAN: 9783337775100

Printed in Europe, USA, Canada, Australia, Japan

Cover: Foto ©ninafisch / pixelio.de

More available books at **www.hansebooks.com**

HISTORICAL REVIEW

OF THE

BOSTON BIJOU THEATRE,

WITH THE

ORIGINAL CASTS OF ALL THE OPERAS

THAT HAVE BEEN PRODUCED AT THE BIJOU, AND

With Photographs Illustrative of the various Scenes in them.

Presented to the Patrons of the Bijou Theatre, April 21st, 1884,

BY THE PUBLISHER,

EDWARD O. SKELTON, General Advertising Agent.

OFFICE, WITH FORBES LITHOGRAPH COMPANY, 181 Devonshire Street, Boston, Mass.

TO THE PATRONS OF THE BIJOU.

~~~~~~~~~

AS is now generally known, the Bijou was the first theatre to be illuminated by the aid of the Electric Light, and the use of that light has enabled the publisher of this review to present to the public photographs of the various Acts of the Operas which have been produced at the Bijou since its dedication. Besides the faithful portrayal of every detail of the stage setting, they are valuable from the fact, that it is the first time that the setting of a series of stage scenes have, as a whole, ever been successfully photographed. This has been done by Mr. N. L. Stebbins of the Blair Tourograph Co., 471 Tremont Street, Boston, who has devoted much time to the study of Photography in its special branches, and recognizing the fact that the electric light would ultimately become a powerful factor in illuminating the world, he, as an experiment, took the first negative by its aid, of " Iolanthe," when it was first produced at the Bijou. Meeting with such marked success in this, his first effort, he continued to photograph scenes from the various Operas as fast as they were presented, and the result of his labors are grouped within these covers, and it is through Mr. Stebbins' courtesy that the Publisher is enabled to present these beautiful Photographs to the patrons of the Bijou.

Very respectfully,

EDWARD O. SKELTON.

Publisher.

BOSTON, April 21st, 1884.

MR. EDWARD H. HASTINGS,

President Bijou Theatre Company.

MR. George H. Tyler, the General Manager of the Bijou Theatre, has from his youth, been connected with theatrical affairs. Like many of the prominent professionals of the present day, he received his initiating training and experience in Amateur Dramatics, and not until 1859, at the Boston Museum, on the occasion of a benefit to "Old Spear," as familiarly called, did he make his debut as a professional in "Charles II," as the Earl of Rochester. Connecting himself with travelling combinations he trod the boards until the out break of the civil war, when putting aside the "sock and buskin," he enrolled in the First Massachusetts Infantry, and served his country until the war was brought to a close, when he again entered the theatrical profession, immediately joining the Stock Company, at Woods' Theatre, Cincinnati, where he remained the seasons of 1865-6-7. Then casting his fortune with Laura Keene's New York Comedy Co., as Stage Manager, and ultimately the General Manager of Laura Keene's Chestnut Street Theatre, Philadelphia. This connection extending through the seasons of 1867-8, '69-70.

He was Manager of Mrs. John Wood's London Burlesque Company portion of season of '71.

In 1871-2, he became the Manager of George L. Fox's N. Y. Humpty Dumpty Troupe.

In 1872-3-4, he was the Manager of the Olympic Theatre, New York City.

In 1875, he was Associate Manager with Geo. L. Fox, at the Globe Theatre, New York, and afterwards became a partner with Mr. Fox, and as such made a tour with the Fox Humpty Dumpty Troupe through the United States and Canadas, which being highly successful, was interrupted by the insanity of Mr. Fox, and his compelled retirement from the stage, but associating with him James S. Maffitt and Bartholomew, and afterwards Robert Frazar, Mr. Tyler completed the tour, as it was originally contemplated.

The season of 1876-7, Mr. Tyler associated himself with Mr. Henry E. Abbey, in some of his enterprises, and in 1877-8, assumed the business management of the Gaiety Theatre, in this city.

Seasons of 1878-9, 80-81-82, he was again associated with Mr. Abbey, and became the Acting Manager of the Park Theatre, this city.

In the spring of 1882, Mr. Tyler entered into an arrangement with Mr. Fred Vokes, whereby a new theatre should be opened for the production of light Opera, which, with the proper accessions of scenery and costumes, could not fail to please the public and return a substantial reward. With Mr. Vokes he secured a long lease of the old Gaiety Theatre, but the financial embarrassment of Mr. Vokes soon following, Mr. Tyler associated himself with Mr. Edward H. Hastings, and Mr. T. Nelson Hastings, when a Stock Company, known as the Bijou Theatre Co. was formed ; after months of labor, and the expenditure of thousands of dollars, the doors of the beautiful Bijou Theatre of the present day, were thrown open to the public, and at once the foresight of Mr. Tyler was verified, for since the inauguration of the Bijou, every Opera which has been produced under his management, has proven an unqualified success, making long runs, and being taken from the boards in the height of their success, that new attractions might be presented.

In May, 1883, Mr. Tyler disposed of his interest in the theatre, to the Messrs. Hastings, but returned to the management again in October, and has since had the entire direction of its affairs.

MR. GEORGE H. TYLER,

General Manager, Bijou Theatre.

To the Gentlemen Patrons of the Bijou.

FROM this date all gentlemen are politely requested to appear in full evening dress at all entertainments occuring in the evening The full dress being especially requested for the Opera. Your dress-coat should be faced with a ribbed silk, either to the button-holes, or the extreme edge. Your dress waist-coat may be either a black embroidered one, or a white corded piquet; the trowsers may be made plain, or braided on the side seams with a military silk braid, or a very fine cord. A standing collar made high, and either straight in front or with the points slightly broken; and for tie, a small black silk one, made up with strap and buckle, and catch for the stud in front, is considered the preferable style—the white ties being reserved for weddings; for gloves wear a pearl color, with black embroidered backs. If any gentleman objects to wearing the full evening suit, he may wear a black diagonal morning coat and waist-coat, with trowsers the same, or of some quiet stripe; or a half dress suit made from worsted, in wine, brown, claret, or blue, but under no circumstances should he wear a business suit, or sack coat.

Advice on matters of dress cheerfully given, goods willingly shown, and samples of work displayed to any who appreciate fine work, and choice styles of goods, at moderate prices.

We never advertise in the regular way, as we do not cater to the masses, but would respectfully invite any reader of this article to call at No. 4 Park Street.

FRANK D. SOMERS, Tailor.

THE BOSTON BIJOU THEATRE

Its History, Past and Present

THE BOSTON BIJOU THEATRE, the most cosy, the most comfortable, and certainly considering its capacity, the most costly, establishment devoted to the Muses in this city, has a history of its own which cannot fail to prove interesting to the patrons of dramatic and musical entertainments, as well as to the general reader.

As long ago as 1835—now forty-nine years since—a theatre existed on this very spot, and the walls of the Bijou are the original walls of the old Lion Theatre. The site was formerly that of the old Lion Tavern, which with its neighbor, the Lamb Tavern (the site of which is now covered by the elegant new hotel adjoining the theatre), were in their day two of the most noted hostleries of the city, and so closely were they situated, that it might be said without impropriety that the Lion and the Lamb laid down together. As a tavern the Lion had its day; and in the latter part of the year 1835, a number of New York gentlemen, at the head of whom was Mr. James Raymond, purchased the estate on Washington Street, and at once commenced the erection of

The Lion Theatre

in rear of the wooden building, which had a frontage upon the street. A number of workmen were employed in the destruction of the old, and the erection of the new building; and so magical, as it were, was the progress made, that on the evening of Monday, January 11th, 1836, the theatre was thrown open to the public. The Lion was built on a novel plan, the intention being to permanently combine equestrian with dramatic entertainments. Those who notice the size of the Bijou Theatre can at once imagine how much space was afforded for a proper representation of the dual entertainments. The interior of the house was neatly but plainly arranged, yet in severe contrast to the gorgeousness which flashes upon the patron of the Bijou. A ring for equestrian performances occupied the place of the then popular pit, corresponding to the orchestra chairs of the present day, while the pit extended under the boxes, of which there were three tiers, and shallow ones at that. The stage proper for dramatic representations occupied the position it does at present. The decorations were by a famous scenic painter of the time, Thomas Reinagle. A drop curtain representing " Bonaparte Crossing the Alps," from the pencil of Robert Jones, the famous artist of the

Send for book on "CARE AND FEEDING OF INFANTS."

DOLIBER, GOODALE & CO., 41 and 42 Central Wharf, BOSTON, MASS.

Tremont Theatre, was looked upon as a marvellous achievement, and it could not have been otherwise than good, as Jones was one of the best scenic artists ever in Boston. The dramatic company was made up of well-known actors and actresses of the day. William Barrymore was the director of the corps, which included Messrs. Durivage, Herbert, Mestayer, Knapp and Houp, and Mesdames Barrett, Mestayer, Eberle, Whittemore, Hurlcy, and Monier. Mr. Buckley was the director of the equestrian business, and among the more prominent of the performers were J. and T. Nathans, Robinson, Dickinson, Perez, Wilmot, Bryant, and Roine. The opening entertainment consisted of a prize address, written by a Mr. T. M. Devon ($50 having been paid for the composition), spoken by Miss Monier. This was followed by Buckstone's "Opera House;" then came the circus business; and the whole concluded with "The Lady of the Lions," a travestic on Bulwer's famous "Lady of Lyons," which had been produced but a short time previous. During the season, Mr. George Ingersoll, a young tragedian, a native of Charlestown, and the celebrated Mrs. Hamblin appeared. During the lady's engagement, a spectacular piece "The Jewess" was brought out, at a great expense, in which the entire stud of horses, elephants, dromedaries, and camels was utilized. Other equestrian pieces followed, with great success, and the first season was brought to a close in April. Shortly after, the theatre was re-opened by Barrymore, and on the 16th of May, that famous actor, the elder Booth, appeared, and the theatre was again closed at the end of his engagement. During the summer the old building in front was pulled down, and brick stores erected, and some alterations were made in the interior of the theatre. The second season was commenced on November 7th, with the same style of entertainments as given during the first season, and was continued until April, 1837, when the house was offered for sale or to let. In June

Cook's Celebrated London Circus Company

leased the theatre, and gave what were probably the best equestrian entertainments ever witnessed in Boston. Messrs. C. R. Thorne, Sen., and Houpt next took a hand at the management, and engaged that budding but remarkable tragedian, Charles H. Eaton, whose melancholy and untimely death at Pittsburg, Pa., on the 4th of June, 1843, was long deplored. The season was a very short-lived one, and again was the theatre closed and offered for sale. This was the year of the great financial panic, which proved disastrous to many a well-established merchant, while dramatic establishments throughout the entire country were very great sufferers. The theatre remained closed until October, 1838, when it was opened by the father of Miss Jean Margaret Davenport (now Mrs. General Lander), then "the infant phenomenon," who played (or a brief season in her specialties, such as "Little Pickle," "The Four Mowbrays," "Lady Teazle," "Richard the Third," and so on. After this, Mr. John Redman, a well-known builder and capitalist, now deceased, made purchase of the theatre, and converted it into what he was pleased to call a

SOMETHING ENTIRELY NEW!!!

Thoroughly Waterproof Garments

Very light, strong, and serviceable, made similar to the celebrated "Mackintosh" garments, but lighter, stronger, and with the advantage of never becoming stiff. The accompanying sample is the material from which the garments are made, and consists of a fine wool cashmere on the outside, a light but strong cambric on the inside, with rubber between.

MADE IN

Mens' Coats,
Boys' Coats,
Mens' Leggins,
Boys' Leggins,
Misses' Circulars,

MADE IN

Ladies' Circulars,
Ladies' Newports,
Misses' Newports,
or Cloth can be purchased
by the yard,
——(One yard wide.)——

CAUTION.

These garments have met with such favor as to cause certain parties to attempt to imitate them. By making an exact copy, even to the manner of putting on the loop, and style of boxing, they have succeeded in making a garment similar in looks but lacking *all* the desirable qualities. In purchasing, be sure the name, "Hall Rubber Mills," is on the loop and you will get the genuine and best waterproof garment of the present day.

HALL RUBBER CO.,
52 & 54 SUMMER STREET, CORNER ARCH STREET.

Mechanics Institute,

in which concerts and other kindred entertainments were given, and in which, for the first time in the city, the ravishing strains of Ole Bull's violin were heard. Shortly after this, the Handel and Hayden Society, which had been giving its oratories in the hall over the Boylston Market, took a lease of the premises, and the name of the building was changed to

The Melodeon

The first oratorio performance was given on the 29th of December, 1839, when "The Messiah" was produced. During week nights the hall was left for miscellaneous entertainments. In 1844, one Leander Rodney who was the agent of the great tragedian W. C. Macready, leased the Melodeon for a brief season, and, fitting it up with scenery, turned it into a temporary theatre. Performances were given on four evenings a week, and the tragedian was assisted by Charlotte Cushman, J. Ryder, W. Wheatley, Wyzeman Marshall, J. B. Fuller, and others, altogether forming one of the finest dramatic companies ever got together in this city. Not long after this the property fell into the hands of Mr. Eliphalet Baker, who enlarged it, and such was its acoustic qualities that it was selected by Jenny Lind, Henrietta Sonntag, Marietta Albomi, Madam Anna Bishop, and other great musical celebreties, in which to give their concerts, and it was also sought after as a most eligible hall in which to display panoramas. On the decease of Mr. Baker, " The Melodeon " passed into the hands of the proprietors of the Boston Theatre. A door of communication was cut between the two buildings, and whenever a grand ball was given in the Theatre, the Melodeon was devoted to the purposes of a supper room. When the great fair in aid of the Sanitary Commission was given in the theatre, the other building, in connection therewith, was used for a series of amateur dramatic performances by a number of well-known ladies and gentlemen of Boston, and the receipts therefrom helped greatly to swell the funds of the Commission. The theatre proprietors having no further use for the property disposed of it to the Hon. Charles Francis Adams, its present proprietor. Some seven years ago, Mr. Adams leased the hall proper to Mr. Jason Wentworth, who again converted it into a theatre, naming it

The Gaiety

Mr. Wentworth held possession of it for several seasons, giving a series of light operatic and dramatic entertainments. But little attention was paid to the production of pieces in general, and as a result the speculation did not prove so profitable as was anticipated. About the close of the year 1881, Mr. George H. Tyler, the manager of the Park Theatre, and Mr. Frederick Vokes, of the well-known and ever popular Vokes Family, formed a co-partnership to establish

The Bijou

The lease of Mr. Wentworth did not expire until the September following, and they secured a lease of the Gaiety, from that expiration, for a
term of years. They immediately went to work perfecting their plans,
for the most complete and elegant theatre of its size, and for the purposes
to which it was intended to devote it, to be found in the United States,
if not, indeed, in the world. In the summer following, the unexpired
term of Mr. Wentworth's lease was secured, and a commencement was
made in earnest. At the same time they secured all the premises over
the stores in front, which had been annexed to the Adams House and
used as lodging rooms. The interior of the theatre building was com-
pletely destroyed, nothing being left but the bare walls, which were greatly
increased in height and a new roof built. At this juncture, Mr. Vokes
became involved in financial difficulties, and he was obliged to relinquish
his share in the co-partnership. Mr. Tyler, pertinacious, and strong in
his belief in the success of the scheme, looked about him for other
assistance, which he found in the persons of T. N. and E. H. Hastings,
two young gentlemen who had not only a sufficiency of means, but an
abiding faith in the future of the enterprise, and a willingness to use that
means to the utmost in making of that future a genuine and unquestioned
success. A co-partnership was formed, and new life was at once infused
into the project. The plans of the theatre having been matured and
perfected by eminent architects, bricklayers, plasterers, carpenters,
painters, decorators, and others, were set to work in great numbers,
and the new and beautiful theatre seemed to grow in beauty as
well as in rapidity, like the "palace of Aladdin, until at length
on Monday evening, December 11th, 1882, when its doors were
opened to the public, the overwhelming audience present was fairly
dazzled by the beauty of the scene, both before and behind the curtain,
It may be said here that it lacked exactly one month of being forty-seven
years from the time of the opening of the Lion, to the opening of the Bijou.
In February, 1883, Mr. Tyler disposed of his interest to the Brothers
Hastings, who are now the sole proprietors of this most beautiful temple
of the drama.

It is unnecessary here to enter upon a sketch of the building.
It stands as a monument to itself, and it has met with, as it
richly deserves, the public approbation. It is the intention of the
proprietors to make it the legitimate home of Parlor Opera in this
country, and to this end they pledge their every effort. The success of
the past, brief as that past has been, foreshadows the future triumphant
career of THE BIJOU.

THE BIJOU THEATRE WAS DEDICATED

December 11, 1882,

BY

Collier's Standard Opera Company

IN

GILBERT & SULLIVAN'S ORIGINAL COMIC OPERA,

ENTITLED,

IOLANTHE;

OR,

THE PEER AND THE PERI,

Which continued as the attraction until April 19th, 1883, having 151 representations. At repeated requests from the public, this Opera was
again placed on the boards from June 4 to June 9, making 8
additional representations.

CAST OF CHARACTERS:

THE LORD CHANCELLOR...... ....Mr. H. E. DIXEY
STREPHON..Sig. BROCOLINI
THE EARL OF TOLLOLLER...................... ....Mr. W. H. FESSENDEN
THE EARL OF MOUNT ARARAT...............Mr. EDWARD P. TEMPLE
PRIVATE WILLIS.................... ....Mr. GUSTAVE KAMMERLEE
THE TRAIN BEARER ....Mr. JAMES H. FINN
IOLANTHE ....Miss CLARA POOLE
PHYLLIS.................... ....Miss JANET EDMONDSON
THE FAIRY QUEEN................................ ....Miss M. A. SANGER
CELIA ..,................. ....Miss ANNIE CALLOWAY
LELIA .... Miss HATTIE DELARO
FLETA ....Miss SYLVIA GERRISH

Grand Chorus of Peers and Fairies; Knights of the Garter, Thistle,
St. Patrick, &c.

LADIES' COSTUMES

— AND —

OUTSIDE GARMENTS.

It is now generally conceded that the large and convenient *Parlor Store* of

THOMAS F. DOHERTY & CO.,

453 WASHINGTON STREET, (FOURTH DOOR FROM WINTER STREET.) BOSTON.

affords the finest opportunity ever offered for the *Ladies* of *New England* to examine, try on, be fitted to, and purchase

DRESSES, COSTUMES, WRAPS, MANTLES,

JACKETS, NEWMARKETS, JERSEY WAISTS,

AND OTHER OUTSIDE GARMENTS.

The *COTTON UNDERWEAR DEPARTMENT* contains the choicest assortment of new and well-made goods ever shown in the city, and *Hand Embroidered French Goods* are a great *Specialty*, at prices but a little higher than the Domestic *Article*.

In the *INFANT DEPARTMENT* everything that a fond mother could think of, from a *Tiny Sock* to the Elaborate Embroidered *Cloak* or Christening *Robe* can be found.

IOLANTHE. Act. I.

ESTABLISHED 1843.

WOODWARD AND BROWN.

MANUFACTURERS OF

GRAND,— —

— SQUARE.-

UPRIGHT

PIANO-FORTES.

SALESROOM:

175ᴬ TREMONT STREET,

(EVANS HOUSE.)   BOSTON, U.S.A.

Monday Eve., April 19, 1883.

———•———

——COLLIER'S——

STANDARD OPERA COMPANY

PRODUCED FOR THE FIRST TIME ON ANY STAGE, THE NEW

SATIRICAL COMIC OPERA,

POUNCE ✦ & ✦ CO.

OR, CAPITAL versus LABOR.

WHICH HELD THE BOARDS UNTIL JUNE 2d, WITH A TOT. L OF 52
REPRESENTATIONS, AND

WITH THE FOLLOWING CAST OF CHARACTERS.

THOMAS POUNCE, the Head of the Firm of Pounce & Co., Mr. E. P. TEMPLE
GEORGE SPOKE, Captain of the Bicycle Club........ Mr. W. H. FESSENDEN
PHILIP TYRE............ } of the Bicycle Club { .. Mr. A. KAMMERLEE
REGINALD HUBBE..... } { ...Mr. HENRY AMBERG
ARTHUR DOBBINS, otherwise Lord Alfred Peerage....Mr. HARRY PEPPER
OLIVER GRIP, a Man for a' that ....Sig. BROCOLINI
JACK SPINDLE, a Son of Toil, contented ....Mr. H. F. FAIRWEATHER
DIGGORY RUGGS .... } { ... Mr. ANDREW METZGER
DICK MUGGS............ } Sons of Toil, { ....Mr. JOHN P. SAVAGE
JACK TUGGS............ } discontented, { ....Mr. EDWARD AIKEN
NED SLUGGS......... ...} { .... Mr. D. P. STEELE

———AND———

WILLIAM CRANK, the Silent Partner. .... Mr. HENRY E. DIXEY
POLLY CHROMO........... ....Miss GERTRUDE FRANKLIN
ELEANOR .... } { .. Miss JANET EDMONDSON
SYLVIA................ } Daughters of { .....Miss SYLVIA GERRISH
MILICENT.. ....} Pounce, { .... Miss IDA ABELL
ESTHER............ .....} { .....Miss HATTIE DELARO
LAURA .... } Daughters of { ...Miss MADELEINE DIXON
OLIVIA .... } Crank, { ....Miss EMMA CALEF
IPHIGENIA .... } { .. .Miss JENNIE McNULTY
ANTIGONE.... .... } { .... Miss RUTH STETSON
ANDROMACHE .... } Nieces of { ....Miss MAY STEELE
MEDEA .... } Pounce, { ...Miss ESTELLE JENNESS
JOCASTA............... .. } { .... Miss FANNIE KNIGHT
ELECTRA .... } { ....Miss EDITH ABELL

THE BOSTON HERALD is the only newspaper in Boston whose circulation is regularly and conspicuously printed at the head of its columns. This custom its proprietors have followed since the time when its circulation was less than 60,000. They have never found it expedient or necessary to pay for the publication of articles of news (?) chronicling in general terms "enormous gains," or gains in percentage. They have never found it necessary to state the circulation in any way, except by simple, direct, actual figures. The enormous circulation of the *Daily Herald* and of the *Sunday Herald* has been earned by honest merit ; by a lavish expenditure of money in obtaining and publishing the most complete news reports, and the best editorial thought ; by an adequate perception of what matter the intelligent reading public desires to read ; by absolute independence in political and religious discussions.

POUNCE & CO. Act I.

Forbes Co., Aberdeen

JUNE 11 TO JUNE 30, 1883.

TWENTY-FOUR REPRESENTATIONS,

COLLIER'S

STANDARD OPERA CO.

Produced for the first times in this city, Gilbert & Sullivan's delightful
musical absurdity, in 2 Acts, entitled the

SORCERER

By special arrangement with R. D'Oyly Carte, London, which was
presented with

Arthur Sullivan's Original Orchestration, Correct and Beautiful Costumes
from London, and the following

CAST OF CHARACTERS.

JOHN WELLINGTON WELLS, first time..... . ...Mr. HENRY E. DIXEY
        (Of J. W. Wells & Co., Family Sorcerers.)
DOCTOR DALY, Vicar of Ploverleigh) ....Mr. DIGBY BELL
        (His first appearance with this company.)
SIR MARMADUKE POINTDEXTRE, an Elderly Baronet .Sig. BROCOLINI
ALEXIS, of the Grenadier Guards—his Son..... ......Mr. W. H. FESSENDEN
NOTARY.............................. ...... Mr. GEO. A. SCHILLER
        (His first appearance with this company.)
LADY SANGAZURE, a lady of ancient lineage, first time,
                      Miss AUGUSTA ROCHE
ALINE, her Daughter—betrothed to Alexis ....Miss JANET EDMONDSON
MRS. PARTLET, a Pew-Opener......................Miss LIZZIE BURTON
CONSTANCE, her Daughter ... .Miss SYLVIA GERRISH
        GRAND CHORUS OF PEASANTRY.

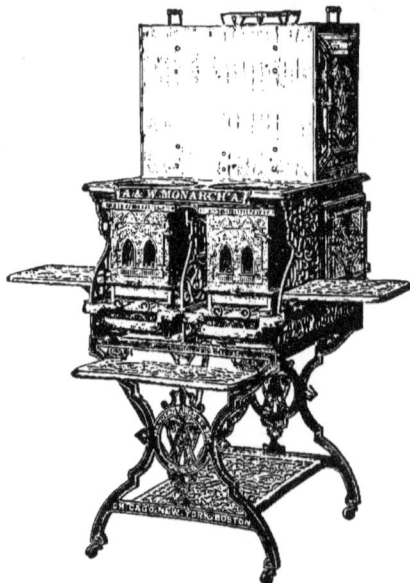

JULY 2D, TO JULY 7TH, 1883.

(EIGHT REPRESENTATIONS.)

— — • • — —

COLLIER'S —

Standard Opera Co.

PRODUCED

GILBERT AND SULLIVAN'S CHARMING OPERA,

PATIENCE

— — • • • —

CAST OF CHARACTERS.

REGINALD BUNTHORNE ....HENRY E. DIXEY
ARCHIBALD GROSVENOR.......................................DIGBY BELL
COL. CALVERLY...... .... RODERT EVANS
MAJOR MARGATROYD.....................................GEORGE A. SCHILLER
LIEUT., The Duke of Dunstable........................ ...HARRY PEPPER
THE SOLICITOR ....JAMES H. FINN
LADY ANGELA...SADIE MARTINOT
LADY ELLA...FANNY RICE
LADY SAPHYR............... ....SYLVIA GERRISH
LADY JANE............... ....AUGUSTA ROCHE
PATIENCE... ....ELLA MAY HUNT

JULY 9TH, 1883 TO JULY 14.

— ·····

COLLIER'S

Standard Opera Company,

PRODUCED

AUDRAIN'S CHARMING OPERA,

THE MASCOT

— · —

CAST OF CHARACTERS.

LORENZO XVII, Prince of Piompino,.................... ....HENRY E. DIXEY

PIPPO,.................................. ....SETH M. CRANE

FREDERICK, Prince of Pisa............ ....HARRY PEPPER

ROCCO.............................. ....GEORGE A. SCHILLER

PARAFANTI...H. F. FAIRMATHER

MARTHEO... ....A. E. EDGAR

COURT PHYSICIAN......... .. .. EDWARD AIKEN

BETTINA, The Mascot...............................,..................ROSE STELLA

FIAMETTA.....................................,....................SADIE MARTINOT

Collateral Loan Co.,

TRANSCRIPT BUILDING,

328 WASHINGTON ST., BOSTON, MASS.

This Corporation, founded by philanthropic citizens of Boston, to loan money on pledge of personal property, at the lowest rates of interest, consistent with self-support, has now been in active operation for over twenty-five years, and has amply fulfilled the expectation of its founders. It furnishes a place of security for valuables, where borrowers of large or small sums are alike sure of strictly honorable and generous treatment, and every indulgence possible is granted its patrons.

This Institution is the friend of the borrower, and assists him in all possible ways to redeem pledges and not deprive him of them, as is too often the custom of pawn-brokers and professional money-lenders.

It is the only Company chartered under the laws of Massachusetts, which loans money on

DIAMONDS, WATCHES, SILVER-WARE, CLOTHING,

AND ALL KINDS OF PERSONAL PROPERTY,

and being under the supervision of the Savings Bank Commissioners, and also Directors appointed by the Governor of the State, and Mayor of the City, every right of the borrower is fully protected.

ALL TRANSACTIONS ARE STRICTLY CONFIDENTIAL.

Many irresponsible persons have taken as much of our incorporate name as they can legally do, with the intention of misleading the public, and great care should be taken to secure the proper address, *for there is but one* Collateral Loan Company, and it has no branch offices. All desired information will be cheerfully given and correspondence solicited.

July 16th to July 28th, 1883.

[SIXTEEN REPRESENTATIONS.]

COLLIER'S

Standard ‡ Opera ‡ Company

Produced in a style of great completeness, Stephens & Solomon's

operatic extravaganza, in two Acts, entitled,

Virginia,

Or, Ringing the Changes.

Music by...EDWARD SOLOMON
Libretto by...HENRY P. STEPHENS

Cast of Characters:

SAMUEL NUBBLES a Navvy... ....Mr. DIGBY BELL
(His original character.)
NICHOLAS DE VILLE, a mysterious personage.........Mr. D. R. GRAHAM
PAUL PLANTAGENET, a Gamekeeper, in love with Virginia,
Mr. W. H. FITZGERALD
ROBINSON BROWN JONES, an unfortunate Railway Guard,
Mr. GEORGE C. BONIFACE, JR.
SIGNOR MACARONI, a prominent Photographer....Mr. GEO. A. SCHILLER
VILLAGE POSTMASTER-GENERAL of the Department, Mr. EDW. AIKEN
VIRGINIA SOMERSET, a Keeper of Geese.........Miss MINNIE CONWAY
LADY MAGNOLIA, a Landed Proprietress...Miss GENIE HOLTZMEYERS
MISS COWSLIP, a Farmeress ....Miss AUGUSTA ROCHE
AMY, the Grocer's Daughter................. ....Miss FANNIE RICE
ALICE, the Butcher's Daughter..........................Miss PERLE DUDLEY
MILDRED, the Bookseller's Daughter.................Miss SYLVIA GERRISH
Peasants, Milkmaids, Navvies, Butchers, &c., &c.

JULY 30, 1883, TO AUGUST 4,

Under the Management of Mr. JOHN J. BRAHAM, who was for

that time Lessee of the Bijou Theatre,

MR. NAT. C. GOODWIN, Jr.

PRESENTED EIGHT TIMES

THE ✦ MASCOT!

CAST OF CHARACTERS,

LORENZO XVII., Prince of Piompino............................NAT. C. GOODWIN, Jr.
PIPPO...SETH McCRANE
FREDERICK, Prince of Piza..............................AUGUSTA ROCHE
ROCCO..GEO. A. SCHILLER
PARAFANTI..H. F. FAIRMARTIN
MARTHEO ....A. E. EDGAR
COURT PHYSICIAN................................EDWARD AIKEN
BETTINA, The Mascot..............................ROSE STELLA
FIAMETTA..FANNY RICE

FALL RIVER LINE

•——BETWEEN——•

BOSTON,

LOWELL, FITCHBURG, NEW BEDFORD, FALL RIVER, NEWPORT, ALL PRINCIPAL
NEW ENGLAND POINTS, BRITISH PROVINCES AND

NEW YORK,

And the South and West, via Fall River and Newport.

NEW IRON STEAMER "PILGRIM,"

AND SUPERB STEAMERS

"BRISTOL" and "PROVIDENCE,"

Connecting Trains leave Boston from Old Colony Depot, corner South
and Kneeland Streets. Steamers leave New York from Pier 28,
North River, foot of Murray Street.

CONNECTION TO AND FROM BROOKLYN AND JERSEY CITY VIA "ANNEX" STEAMER

Connections made at the latter point with Early Trains for

Philadelphia, Baltimore, Washington and the South and West.

TICKETS, STATEROOMS, BERTHS, Etc.,

SECURED IN BOSTON AT THE LINE OFFICE,

3 Old State House, and The Old Colony Depot.

GEO. L. CONNOR, G. P. A., New York.   J. R. KENDRICK, Gen'l Man'r, Boston.
L. H. PALMER, Agent, 3 Old State House, Boston.

THE PRELIMINARY SEASON OF 1883-4 WAS OPENED

MONDAY, AUGUST 27TH, 1883,

—— BY ——

THE ORIGINAL AND CELEBRATED

RICE'S SURPRISE PARTY,

Mr. EDWARD E. RICE, Sole Proprietor and Manager,

Who appeared thirty two times in the highly sensational, operatic, musical
comedy *melange*, in two Acts, entitled,

POP

Or, The Fortunes of a Dramatic Author,

With the following

CAST OF CHARACTERS.

ADOLPHUS POP, a dramatic author, whose works have not met with
the recognition they deserve ....Mr. JOHN A. MACKAY
ANTHONY BELSIZE, from Alabama, a wealthy Southerner, who is
"never in a hurry;" who used to masquerade in female attire in
his youth ....Mr. G. K. FORTESQUE
CHARLES PAGE, a rising young English attorney, very much in
love with Belle.......................................Mr. N. S. BURNHAM
JEM SMART, alias Asa Jebb, a doubtful character, who would be better
if circumstances were different..................Mr. H. L. RATTENBERRY
KNOUS, a German servant, who wrestles with the vernacular in a most
remarkable manner..... ....Mr. RICHARD GORMAN
SPRIGGINS, a modest office boy, or attorney's clerk, in the employ of
Shary & Lewis............. ....Miss EMMA HANLEY
SOPHIE BELSIZE, niece of Anthony Belsize, a perfect Southern
beauty... ....Miss MARIE JANSEN
BELLE ADAMS, a daughter of Belsize by his first wife, an actress of
the Theatre Royal .... Miss IRENE PERRY
ADELE POP, sister to Adolphus, a ballet dancer and vocalist at the
Royal Alhambra......................... ....Miss MAY STEMBLER
JEANETTE, a French waiting-maid, who loves when she loves, Miss IDA BELL
Sailors, Passengers on the Steamship, etc., by other members of the
Company.

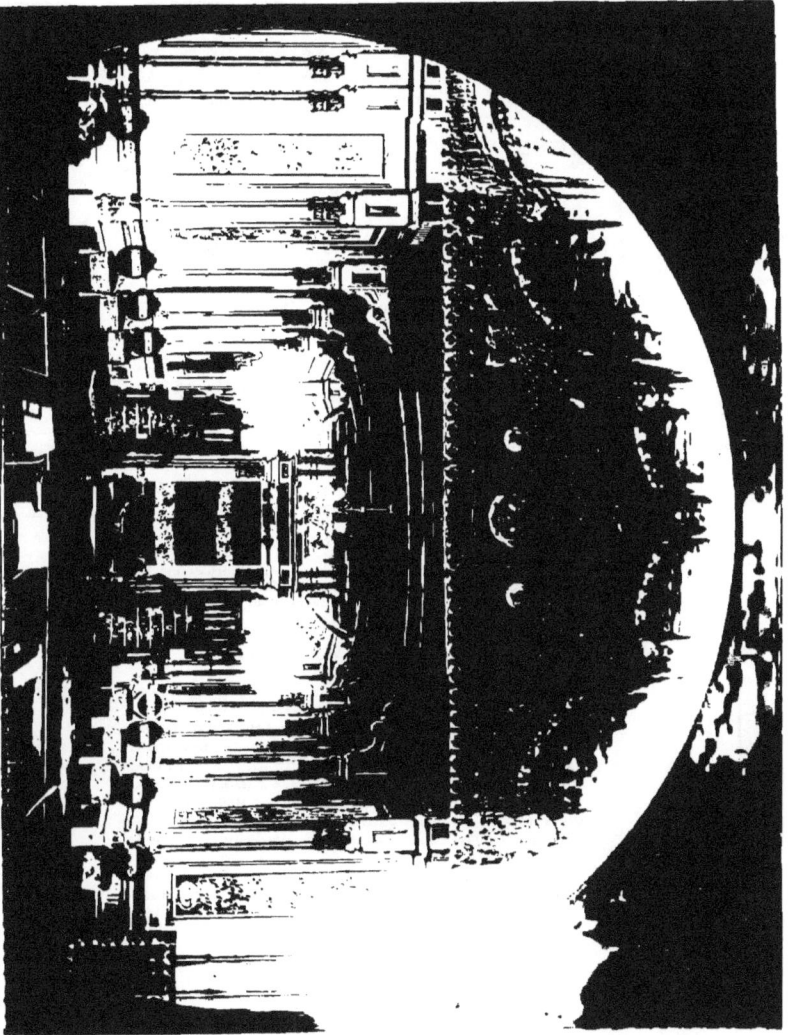

Forbes Co.. Albertype.

POP. Act. II. Grand Saloon Steamer Servia.

THE REGULAR SEASON OF 1883-4 WAS INAUGURATED

MONDAY EVENING, SEPT. 24, 1883,

By the Initial Appearance of

THE BIJOU THEATRE COMIC OPERA COMPANY

IN

Stephens' and Solomon's Masterpiece,

"VIRGINIA,"

By ARRANGEMENT WITH TOWNSEND PERCY, ESQ.,

As Reconstructed by J. CHEEVER GOODWIN,

And which was continued as the attraction until October 10th, a total of 28
representations. October 12th and matinee 13th, the Opera was repeated with Georgine Januschowsky in the title role.

⇢*CAST OF CHARACTERS*⇠

NICHOLAS DE VILLE, a Mysterious Person,............Sig. C. BROCOLINI
(The part originally written for him.)
SAM'L NUBBLES, a Navvy,................................Mr. A. WILKINSON
ROBINSON, BROWN-JONES, a Foundling,.. ......Mr. W. H. FESSENDEN
PAUL MIDDLETON, a Gamekeeper..........................Mr. C. L. WEEKS
SIG. MACARONI, a Photographer............................Mr. W. J. CLARK
THE POSTMAN, a Convenience..............................Mr. E. A. OSGOOD
VIRGINIA, a Keeper of Geese........................Miss JANET EDMONDSON
LADY MAGNOLIA, a Landed Proprietress, ...Miss EMMA C. TUTTLE
SARAH COWSLIP, a Widow.............................Miss CLARA POOLE
AMY, a Grocer's Daughter............ ....Miss HATTIE DELARO
ALICE, a Butcher's Daughter....................... ..Miss AGNES FOLSOME
MILDRED, a Baker's Daughter......................Miss CLARA F. LANE
JACK BOWLINE, with a Hornpipe ....MAY STEELE
PEASANTS, MILKMAIDS, NAVVIES, YOUNGER SONS, &C.

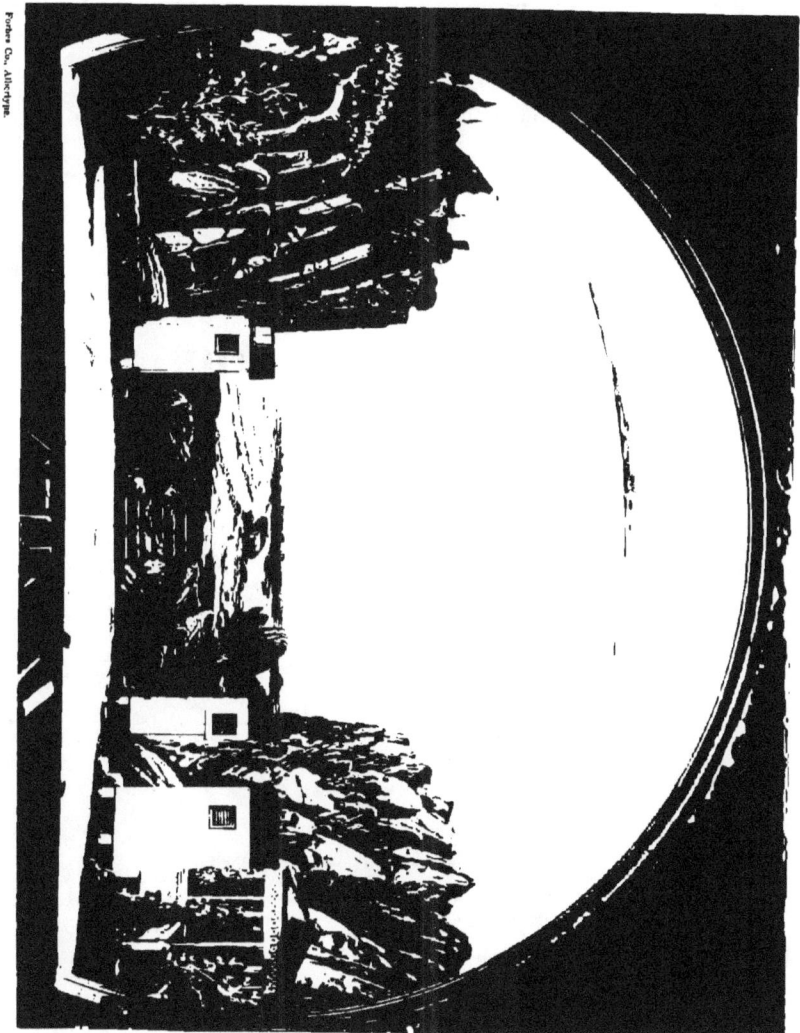

VIRGINIA. Act II.

Forbes Co., Allotype.

OCTOBER 11th & 13th, 1883.

The Bijou Theatre Comic Opera Company

APPEARED IN

GILBERT & SULLIVAN'S

H. M. S. PINAFORE?

❖Cast of Characters❖

SIR JOSEPH PORTER, K.C.B.................................... Mr. A WILKINSON
CAPT. CORCORAN... Mr. C. BROCOLINI
RALPH RACKSTRAW.............................. .. Mr W. H. FESSENDEN
DICK DEADEYE..Mr. F. DANIELS
BOATSWAIN ....Mr. G. KAMMERLEE
MIDSHIPMAN........................... ....MASTER JACQUES
JOSEPHINE........... ....Miss JANET EDMONDSON
LITTLE BUTTERCUP.... ....Miss CLARA POOLE
HEBE...Miss HATTIE DELARO

→TRIAL ❖ BY ❖ JURY←

❖Cast of Characters❖

JUDGE...Mr. FRANK DANIELS
COUNSEL FOR PLAINTIFF ....Mr. A. WILKINSON
DEFENDANT ....Mr. A. BELL
USHER OF COURT.....................................Mr. G. KAMMERLEE
FOREMAN OF JURY... ....Mr. W. W. TUTTLE
PLAINTIFF...................................... ....Miss ROSE STELLA

W. A. SMITH,

No. 383 Washington Street,

OPPOSITE HEAD OF FRANKLIN ST.,

UP STAIRS, ROOM 5,

—IMPORTER OF—

𝔇iamonds and 𝔓recious 𝔖tones,

AND MANUFACTURER OF

Diamond Jewelry.

No. 383 WASHINGTON STREET,

BOSTON.

PINAFORE.

Forbes Co., Albertype.

OCTOBER 15th. 1883,

THERE BEGAN THE BILLIANT ENGAGEMENT OF

MR. CHAS. WYNDHAM,

AND HIS CELEBRATED

COMEDY COMPANY,

From the CRITERION THEATRE, London,

WHICH CONTINUED FOR SIX WEEKS, WITH 48 PERFORMANCES.

The First Week there was Produced

"14 DAYS" and "RUTH'S ROMANCE."

THE SECOND WEEK,

"THE LANCERS."

THE THIRD WEEK,

"The Great Divorce Case, and "Withered Leaves,"

THE FOURTH WEEK,

" Brighton, and The Household Fairy."

THE FIFTH WEEK,

" Pink Dominoes, and The Household Fairy."

THE SIXTH WEEK all the Comedies were repeated on different evenings, excepting " The Lancers," and for that on Friday Evening,
Nov. 24th, which was the occasion of a Complimentary
Benefit to Mr. WYNDHAM, there was produced
for the only time

"Butterfly Fever" and "The Cozey Couple."

◄ NOVEMBER 26, TO DECEMBER 8, 1883. ►

The Bijou Theatre Comic Opera Co.

APPEARED SEVENTEEN TIMES IN

GILBERT AND SULLIVAN'S ORIGINAL COMIC OPERA,

IN TWO ACTS, ENTITLED

IOLANTHE

— OR —

THE PEER AND THE PERI

Which was produced by special arrangement with DOYLE CARTE,
with the following superior

CAST OF CHARACTERS:

THE LORD CHANCELLOR, (first time in America)..ARTHUR WILKINSON
STREPHON.................... ....SIG. BROCOLINI
THE EARL OF TOLLOLLER. ....W. H. FESSENDEN
THE EARL OF MOUNT ARARAT (first appearance here)..HARRY ALLEN
PRIVATE WILLIS..................... .. ,. .. GUSTAVE KAMMERLEE
THE TRAIN BEARER ....J. G. HAMBLIN, Jr
IOLANTHE.. ....CLARA POOLE
PHYLLIS ....JANET EDMONDSON
THE FAIRY QUEEN.................... ....MARY A. SANGER
LELIA...HATTIE DELARO
CELIA. .... AGNES FOLSOME
FLETA............. ....MAY STEELE

Grand Chorus of Peers and Fairies.

IOLANTHE. Act II.

ON THE ANNIVERSARY OF THE OPENING OF THE
BIJOU THEATRE,

Tuesday Evening, Dec. 11th, 1883.

THE BIJOU THEATRE

Comic Opera Company,

Produced for the first time in this city Carl Millocker's European
Operatic Sensation, entitled:

✦ THE BEGGAR STUDENT ✦

Which reached above 150 representations in Vienna and Berlin, and which
continued as the attraction at this Theatre, until February 21st,
1884, receiving 84 representations.

COUNTESS PALMATICA...EDITH ABELL
LAURA.........} her daughters }....GEORGEINE VON JANUSCHOWSKY
BRONISLAVA }....................................ADELAIDE RANDALL
SYMON SYMONOVICZ, the Beggar Student...... ...WM. H. FESSENDEN
JANITSKY, a Polish Noble ....GEO. W. TRAVERNER
GENERAL OLLENDORF, Governor of Cracow,............HARRY ALLEN
LIEUT. POPPENBURG....}   {.... ARTHUR WILKINSON
MAJOR HOLZHOFF........}   {........ALEXANDER BELL
LIEUT. WANGENHEIM..} Saxon Officers, {...........E. A. OSGOOD
LIEUT. SCHWEINITZ.....}   {.......C. L. WEEKS
CAPT. HENRICI...........}   {.............JOS. W. BYRNE
ENSIGN RICHTOFEN.....}   {.........JAS. L. GILBERT
BOGUMIL....... } Cousins of Palmatica {.....GUSTAVE KAMMERLEE
EVA, his wife... }   {........ ....EMMA C. TUTTLE
BURGOMASTER.............. .... E. J. CLONEY
ENTERICH, a jailor.. FRANK DANIELS
PIFFKE........} his assistants }.........................ALEXANDER BELL
PUFFKE....... }   }.......................J. G HAMBLIN, Jr
SITZKA, an inn-keeper..P. STEELE
ONOUPHRIE, servant..J. S H. KNOX
ALEXIS, a prisoner..J. V. SAVAGE

Polish Nobles, Pages, Students, Bridesmaids, Peasants, Children and
Market-people, Hebrew Traders, Lancers, Prisoners and Soldiers,
forming many fine character personations.

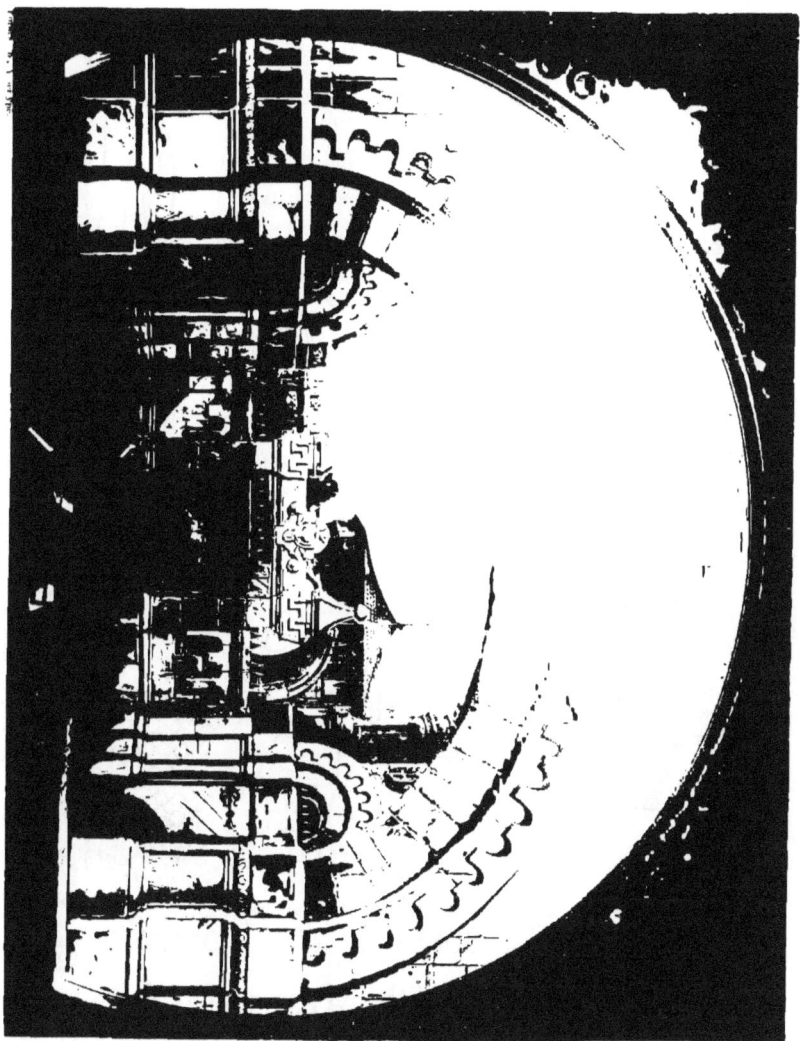

BEGGAR STUDENT. Act I. Scene 1st.

FULL DRESS SUITS.
Cannot be distinguished from Custom Made, at HALF Custom Prices.

PRINCE ALBERT SUITS.
Perfect Fitting and Stylish. In Diagonals, Corkscrews and Fancy Worsteds.

FOUR-BUTTON CUT-AWAY FROCK SUITS.
In all the Latest Shades and Fabrics.

COACHMAN'S LIVERY TOP-COAT.
Light Weight, ... $18.00
Heavy Weight, ... 24.00

CHILDREN'S CLOTHING a Specialty.
VACATION
SCHOOL **SUITS.**
DRESS
All Sizes and all Prices.

Indestructible Suits, All-Wool and Strong
SUPERIOR IN MAKE, STYLE, FIT.
Bring in the Little Folks.

SAILOR SUITS.
FROM THE CHEAPEST TO THE BEST.
XTRA PANTS, BLOUSES, SHIRT WAISTS
In all the New Shades.

J. B. BARNABY & CO., Fashionable Clothiers,
607 & 609 WASHINGTON STREET, opp. Globe Theatre, Boston, Mass.

BEGGAR STUDENT. Act I. Scene 2d.

BEGGAR STUDENT. Act II.

BEGGAR STUDENT. Act III.

FEBRUARY 21, 1884.

THE BOSTON BIJOU THEATRE

Comic Opera Company

Produced FRANZ VON SUPPES'S Latest European Success, the Grand Opera Comique in 3 Acts, entitled,

A TRIP TO AFRICA.

English version by EMIL SCHWAB, adapted and arranged for the English stage by ADOLPH NEUENDORFF.

CAST OF CHARACTERS.

TITANINA FANFANI, the Heiress, GEORGINE VON JANUSCHOWSKY
FANFANI PASHA, her Uncle...................... ....HARRY BROWN
MIRADILLO, an European...................................W. H. FESSENDEN
ANTARSID, Prince of the Maronites, a Christian tribe,...GEO. W. TRAVENNE
TESSA, a young Milliner from Palermo........ ....LILLIE WEST
BUCCAMETTA, her Mother..., ...MAY SYLVIE
PERICLES, Hotel Keeper...........................GUSTAVE KAMMERLEE
NAKID, a Koptic Dealer in Poison and Perfumes.............MURRY WOODS
SEBIL, an Abyssinian Slave................................EMMA C. TUTTLE
HOSH, Servant in Pericles' Hotel...............................J. S. B. KNOX
A MUEZZIN...W. W. TUTTLE
A MARONITE............ ....E. A. OSGOOD
FIRST SAIS....... ....C. L. WEEKS
SECOND SAIS ....C. R. FULLERTON

Maronites, Hotel Servants, Guests of Fanfani Pasha, Slave Traders, Muleteers,
Dancers, Greek and Arabian People.

TIME—THE PRESENT. SCENE FIRST AND SECOND ACTS, CAIRO. THIRD ACT,
THE INTERIOR OF AFRICA.

TRIP TO AFRICA. Act I.

→ QUOTATIONS ←

Ladies' Banking Parlors,

Nos. 6 & 7 EVANS HOUSE,

175 Tremont Street, Boston,

(NEAR BOYLSTON STREET.)

Of all sales of STOCKS, GOVERNMENT BONDS, and other SECURITIES, as soon as made, on the

New York and Boston Exchanges,

This is the only office in Boston devoted exclusively to ladies, furnished and fitted solely for their use, and where all the facilities and accommodations of a down-town office are to be found.

The prices, as soon as received by wire, are posted on a "Bulletin Board," in large figures, thus giving ladies an opportunity of watching the fluctuations of STOCKS and BONDS on the market, on which knowledge they may act at once, thereby avoiding the numerous delays and annoyances frequently met with at other offices. The ladies' branch is connected with the main office by private telephone.

INVESTMENTS.

GOVERNMENT, STATE, CITY, and other first-class investments a specialty.

UNITED STATES GOVERNMENT BONDS cashed or exchanged into other investments without charge.

Stocks and Bonds

Bought and sold for cash, or carried on margin of from 3 to 10 per cent, in large or fractional lots.

ORDERS BY MAIL OR TELEGRAPH RECEIVE PROMPT ATTENTION.

ROBERT J. TABRAHAM & CO.,

BANKERS AND BROKERS,

BOSTON, NEW YORK.

BOSTON OFFICE, . 66 DEVONSHIRE STREET.

TRIP TO AFRICA. Act II.

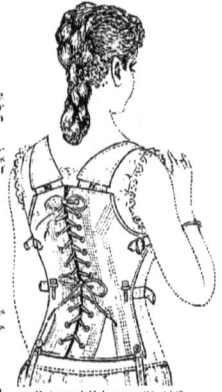

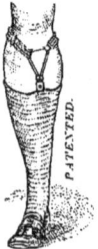

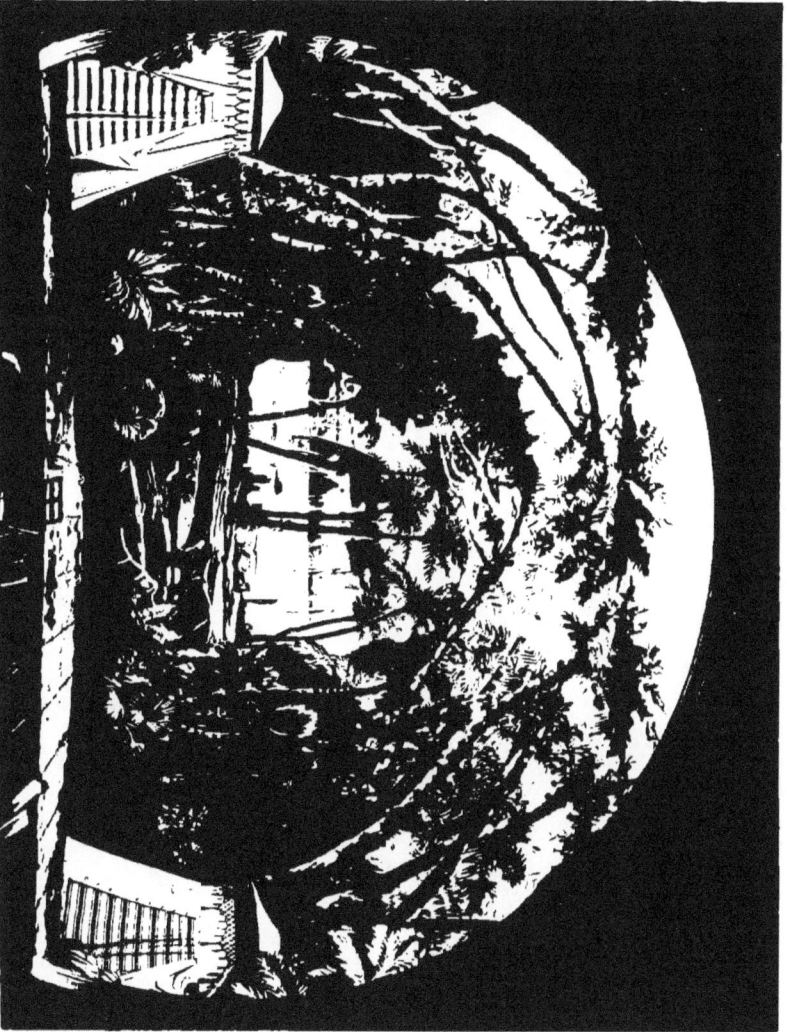

TRIP TO AFRICA.   Act III.